The Joy of Sonatinas

for Piano
In the Early-To-Intermediate Grades
Selected and Edited by Denes Agay

THE JOY OF SONATINAS is a graded collection of sonatinas and suites, in the easy-to-intermediate levels. All selections are in their original forms and are presented complete with all movements of each work.

Included are not only the well-known, favorite sonatinas of the study literature but also numerous other delightful works by Benda, Latour, Glazunov, and others, either rarely encountered, or printed for the first time in the United States.

Two new compositions by Denes Agay, *Little Suite in Baroque Style* and *Sonatina in Classic Style* round out the content of this fine collection, a most valuable addition to the teaching and recital repertory.

Distributed throughout the world by
Music Sales, 257 Park Avenue South, New York, N.Y. 10010, U.S.A.
Music Sales, 8/9 Frith Street, London, W1V 5TZ, England.
Music Sales, 120 Rothschild Avenue, Rosebery, N.S.W. 2018, Australia.

Contents

Sonatina

Three Little Pieces

1

Antonio Diabelli

2

3

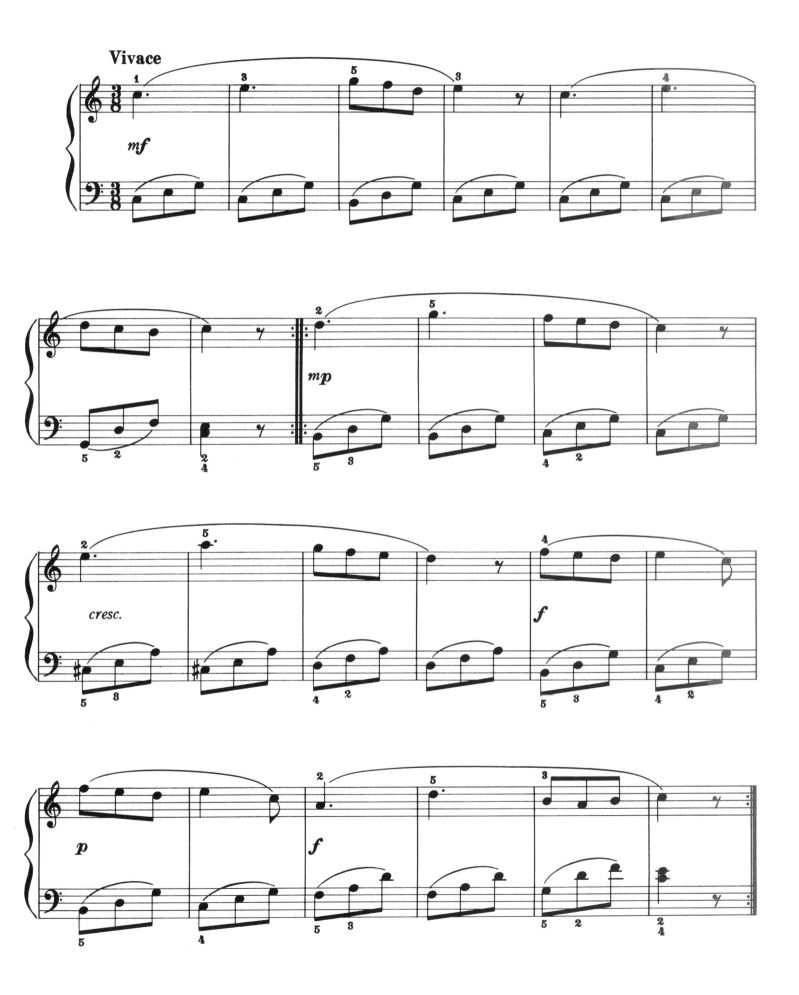

Sonatina

Op. 208 No. 1

Jacob Schmitt

Rondo
Allegretto

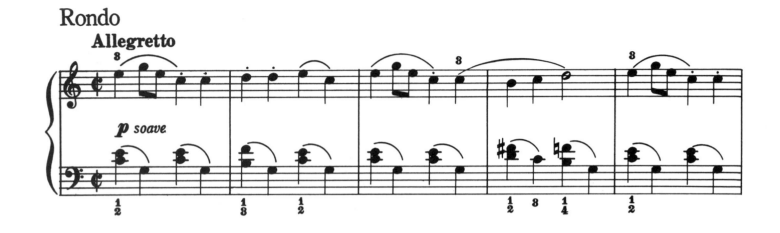

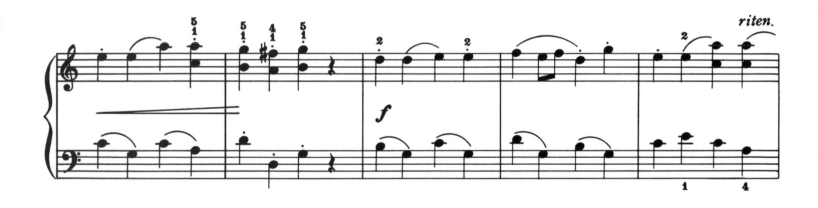

Sonatina

Op. 36 No. 1

Muzio Clementi

Allegro moderato

Andante

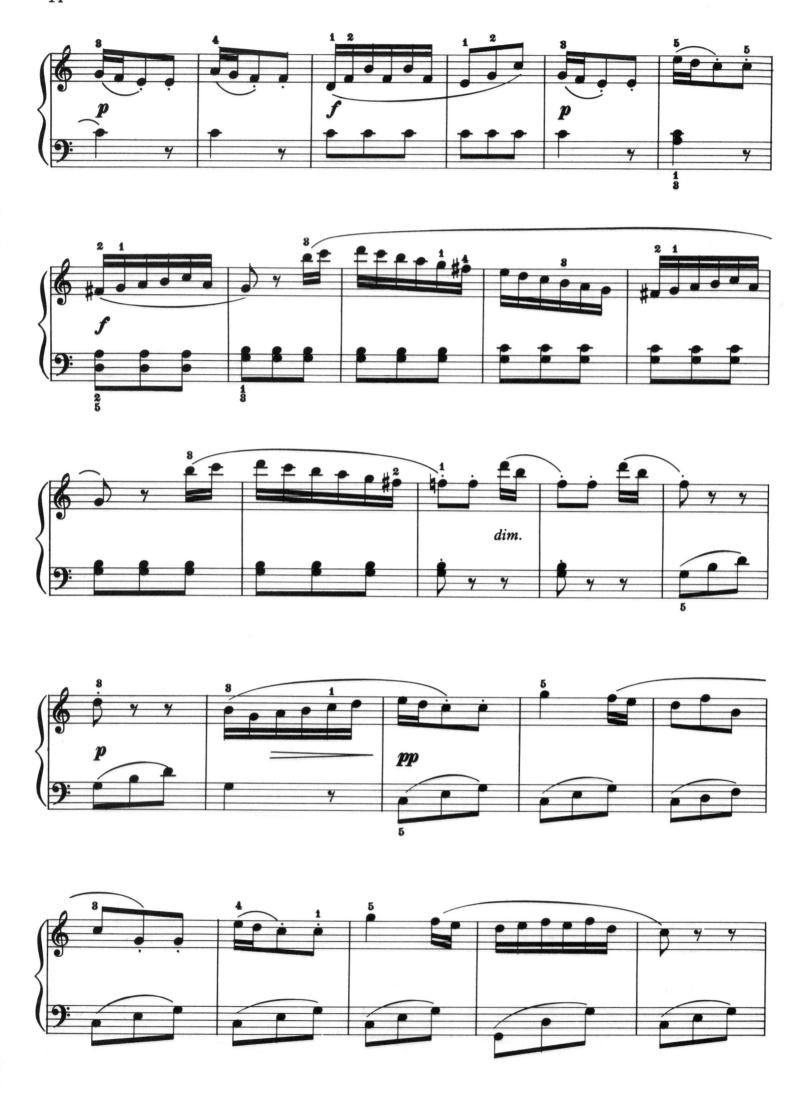

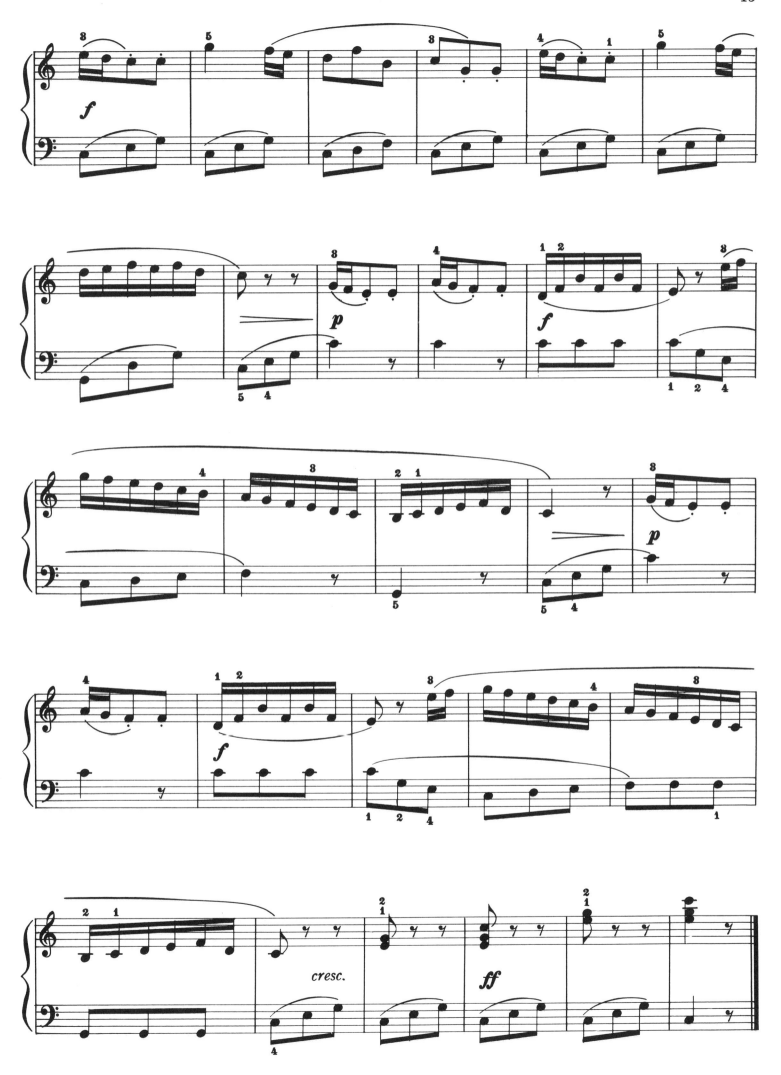

Little Suite in Baroque Style

1. Prelude

Denes Agay

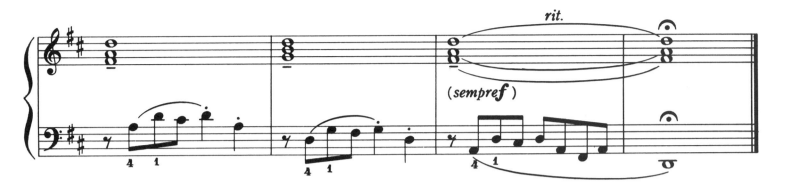

2. Minuet

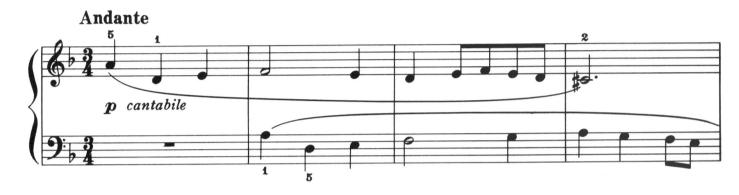

3. Gavotte and Musette

Musette

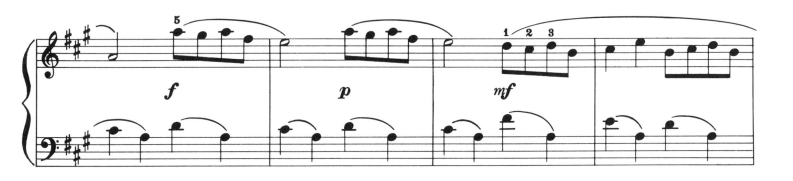

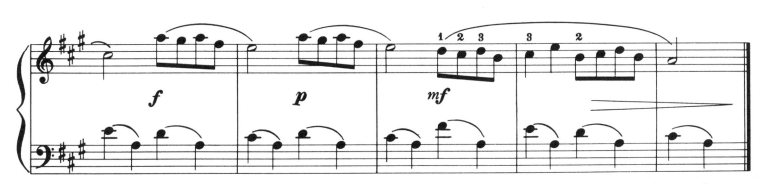

Repeat Gavotte

20

4. Bourrée

5. Gigue

Sonatina

with Tarantella — Op. 157, No. 1

Fritz Spindler

Allegro

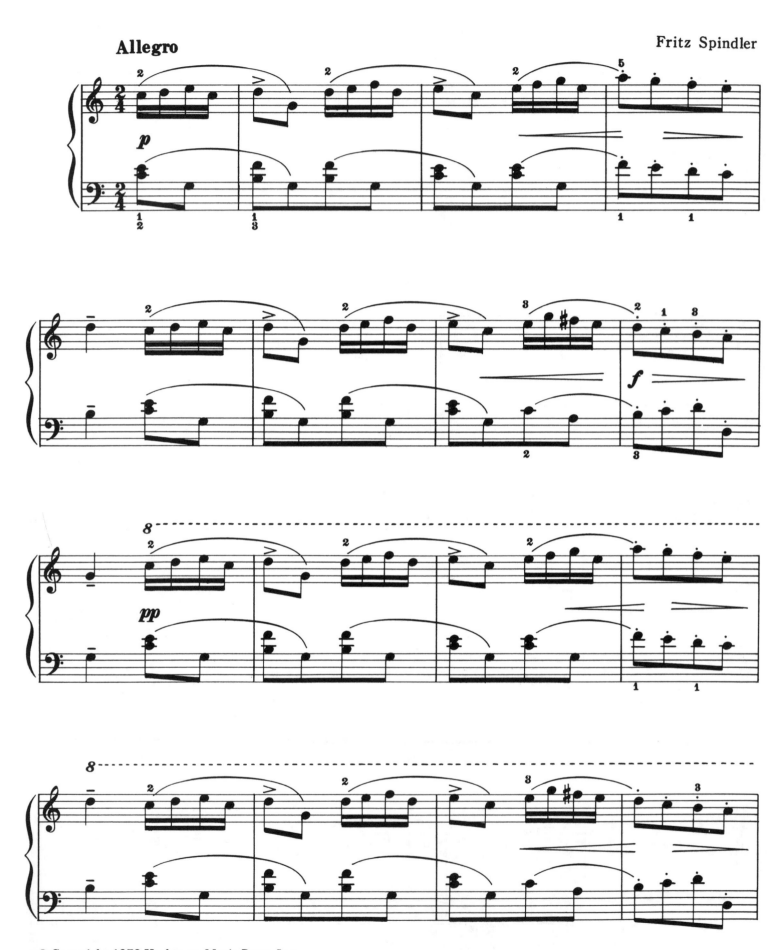

Tarantella

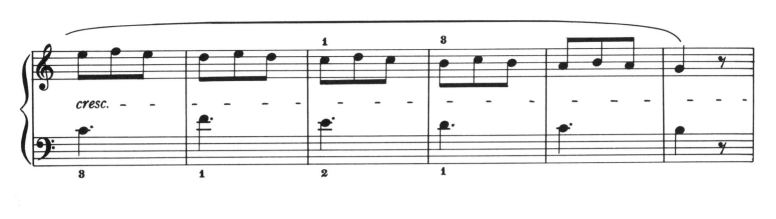

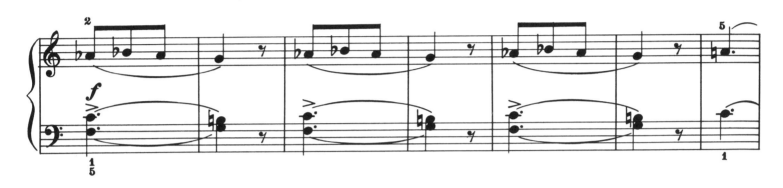

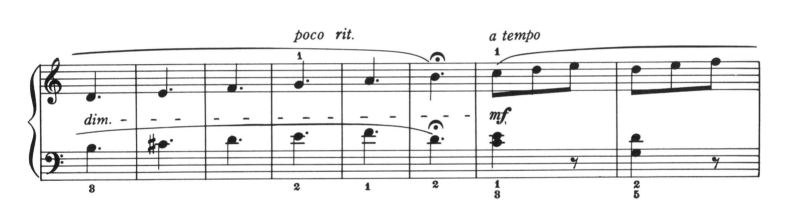

Sonatina

Ludwig van Beethoven

Romanze
Allegretto

Sonatina

Op. 5 No. 1

Konstantin Sorokin

Sonata No. 1

I

Jean T. Latour

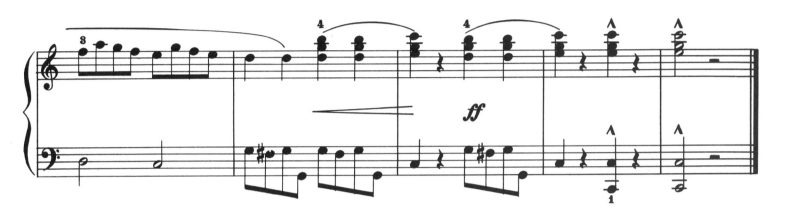

II
Pastorale

III
Rondo

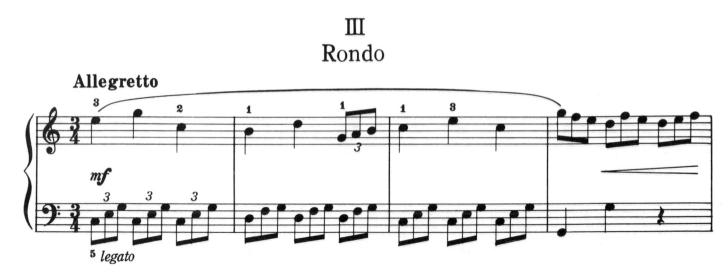

Sonatina

Op. 76, No. 5

Cornelius Gurlitt

Allegro con brio

Allegretto scherzando

Allegro non troppo

Sonatina

F major

Ludwig van Beethoven

Allegro assai

Rondo
Allegro

Circus Sonatina

V. Reiman

Sonatina

Op. 55, No.1

Friedrich Kuhlau

Allegretto

Sonatina

A minor

Jiri Antonin Benda

Sonatina

I

Wolfgang Amadeus Mozart

Coda

II Rondo

Allegro

(legato)

Sonatina in Classic Style

I

Denes Agay

II
Arioso

Lento, con molto espressione ♩ = ca 60

legato sempre

Optional repeat from 𝄋

III
Rondo

Sonatina
Op. 27, No. 16

Dmitri Kabalevsky

Allegretto

Sonatina

Alexander Glazunov

Sonatina

Op. 168, No. 2

Antonio Diabelli

Allegro moderato

Andante sostenuto

a)

78

Rondo
Allegretto

Sonatinetta

Children At Play

T. Nazarova

Lively and cheerful

Printed and bound in Great Britain by
Caligraving Limited Thetford Norfolk